CRICUT MAKER

HANDBOOK (2023)

The Complete User Guide To Master Cricut Maker 3 And Design Space in 45 MINUTES

Shelli Lynne

Table of Contents

CHAPTER ONE... 11

What Is Cricut? 11

Different Types of Cricut Machine.......................12

History Of Cricut Machine 17

Evolutionary Of Cricut Machine; 19

What Can I Make With Cricut?........................... 23

How Does Cricut Machine Work? 24

What Cricut Machines Are Out There Right Now?

....24

CHAPTER TWO...25

Cricut Buying Guide 25

Different Cricut Machines In The Market Today

....27

   Cricut Maker 3:...28

   Cricut Explore 3: 30

Cricut Explore Air 2:.. 31

Cricut Maker:...32

Cricut Joy: 32

Design Space..34

Cheat Sheet...35

CHAPTER THREE...36

Getting Started 36

Unboxing Cricut Maker 3 36

Anatomy of the Cricut Maker 3 41

Initial Setup of Cricut Maker 3......................... 46

CHAPTER FOUR 54

Facts To Consider Before Crafting....................54

Tips To Know Before You Start Crafting............55

Purchase the Right Crafting Materials: 55

Organize your Crafting Space: 57

Familiarize Yourself with the Cricut Machine: 58

Manage your crafting materials: 59

Study the Cheat Sheet: 61

Understand the Design Space: 63

Sort for more information online: 64

Learn from your Mistakes: 65

CHAPTER FIVE 66

Cricut Design Space 66

Importance of Design Space: 66

How to Install Design Space for Desktop 68

How to Install Design Space for iOS device 70

How does the Design Space Look Like on a Desktop? 72

How does the Design Space Look Like on an iOS Device? 73

CHAPTER SIX 74

Cricut Design Space for Beginners 74

Top Panel 74

Edit Panel 75

Design Panel 82

Layers Panel 85

CHAPTER SEVEN 88

Design Space Tips and Tricks 88

How to Link Cartridges in Design Space?......... 88

How to use Color Sync Panel 90

How to Use Patterns in Cricut Design Space..... 92

How to Mirror Designs 94

Working with Text in Design Space 96

How to Modify Text: 96

How to Rotate Text 97

Sizing a Text 97

Resizing the text box 98

Text Wrapping 98

How to Curve Text..99

How to Delete Text...99

Design Space Tips and Tricks 100

CHAPTER EIGHT...103

Cricut Materials 103

Cardstock:...104

Vinyl:..107

Iron-on:.. 109

Fabric: 111

Leather:...113

Paper: 115

CHAPTER NINE 117

Selecting Blades 117

Types of Cricut Blades 118

Fine-Point Blades 118

Premium Fine Point Blade: 119

Deep Point Blade:...119

Bonded-Fabric Blade:...119

QuickSwap Tools 120

Debossing Tip:...120

Perforation Blade:...120

Engraving Tip: 120

Wavy Blade: 121

Scoring and Double Scoring Wheel:...............121

Knife Blade.. 122

Rotary Blade 123

Foil Transfer Tool.. 124

Scoring Stylus 125

How to Change a Knife Blade 126

CHAPTER TEN 127

Maintaining Cricut Maker 3.............................127

How to Clean the Interior of Maker 3................129

CHAPTER ELEVEN 131

Cricut Projects...131

How to make Mugs with Cricut Maker 3..........134

How to Make Stenciled Pillowcases...................137

How to make Custom t-shirts 140

How to make Fabric headbands........................143

How to make Custom invitations 146

What Next? 148

ABOUT BOOK 149

CHAPTER ONE

What Is Cricut?

A cricut is a machine that serves as cutting equipment and mostly uses electricity to perform its work. It is a computer-controlled cutting machine, majorly designed for Crafters, used in cutting materials like papers, fabrics, leather, mat board, wood, and vinyl. It makes cutting easier and faster, providing a neat and desired result.

Cricut machines have brought the solution to some horrible cutting experiences, especially those used to cut large and strong materials. It is to make cutting easier and faster. It can be used in the home, offices, companies, schools, and more to cut different materials.

Every Cricut machine has different material makeup. Therefore, before you can purchase a Cricut machine, there must be a decision on the purpose for which the particular service you want to render with a Cricut machine determines the type and quality of the Cricut machine you'll need to buy.

Different Types of Cricut Machine

Cricut Machines will make your projects easy when it comes to precision cutting, plotting, and crafting. These cutting machines allow you to create all kinds of projects, from paper crafts to vinyl decals. There are different types of Cricut machines and they include;

Cricut Explore Air:

The Cricut Explore Air can accurately cut intricate shapes with various blades for every situation. This machine uses cut smart technology with several pens to perform several results, such as creating fold lines and designing paper materials.

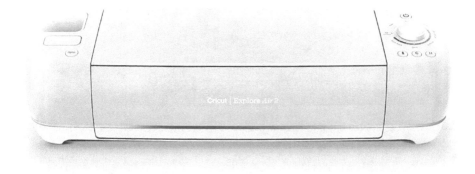

Cricut Maker:

Cricut Maker is one of the best designer machines that uses several tools for cutting, scoring, writing & adding decorative effects. This machine can cut various materials like paper, vinyl, HTV (heat transfer vinyl), and cardstock.

Cricut Expression:

Cricut Create:

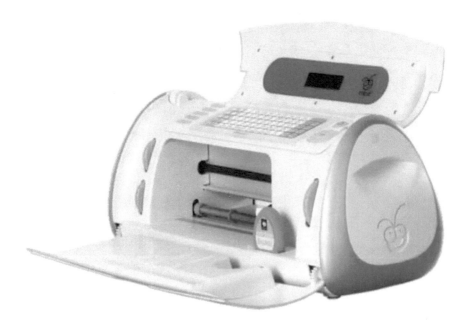

Cricut Explore 2, Cricut Cake, Cricut Personal, Cricut Joy, Cricut Mini, Cricut Imagine, Cricut Explore Air 2.

History Of Cricut Machine

The Cricut machine was manufactured on the 21st day of December 2003, in the city of Utah, by Provo Craft and Novelty, Inc. Before this time, so many other tools had been used over the years to alternate Cricut. However, these tools still needed improvement.

The results still needed to be improved in accuracy and efficacy. So many devices have been invented over the years to solve cutting needs, but most times, using these tools always reminds us that there has to be more to make cutting easier, faster, and more efficient. People like Provo and Novelty began to think of an alternative.

After much research, they came up with the idea to build a machine like Cricut, which will completely eradicate the stress people undergo while cutting and create a possible means of accurately getting the intended result after cutting.

Cricut machine is under the 5th generation, which uses artificial intelligence. It is a modernized tool that gives you your desired shape and generally an intended endpoint.

Evolutionary Of Cricut Machine;

Cricut has undergone several evolution over the years since it was formed. Here are some products that has been released by Cricut;

Cricut Personal Machine: This is used to cut a great variety of paper from vellum to cardstock, up to 0.5mm thick. Cardstock pads and designer paper pads that can merge with the Cricut shape cartridges were also built into this machine. 6×12 papers fit perfectly in the Cricut machine.

Cricut Create: Cricut Create majorly works with an easy-to-use app for designing and personalizing almost anything, including; unique apparel, custom card, and nearly everyday items like poster board, glitter paper, cardboard, sticker paper, iron-on materials, polyester, etc. It comes with a Don Juan cartridge, cartridge binder, keypad overlay, and handbook.

Cricut Cake: This specific Cricut is made of food-safe parts to cut edible materials, such as frosting sheets, gum paste, cakes, fondants, etc. It came out on the 20th of April 2010, works with all cartridges, and is made with a new mat without adhesive from food-grade materials to allow Crisco and vegetable shortening to be put on it.

Cricut Imagine: Cricut Imagine is used to design, print, and cut your creative project to proceed to the next level. Its cartridges are meant to work with the Cricut imagine machine "print then cut" technology.

Cricut Mini: Cricut Mini helps you to cut a wide collection of materials at a whole host of sizes; it cuts fabrics, chipboard, images, and fonts on cardstock. It can also cut foils in small and large sizes. It is basically meant for unusual objects like hard tools, tight, stuffed animals, shoes, etc. The Cricut craft room software can control the Cricut mini. With the Cricut craft room, you can access about 400 free images before purchasing additional ones.

Cricut Expression: This is one of the innovations of Provo Craft, which stand to be among the largest Cricut machines, used in cutting materials from a tiny 1/4 inch up to 23 1/2 inch tall. It can cut vinyl, vellum, fabrics, chipboard, cardstock, etc. The multi-cut function; can also cut fun foam, thick metal sheets, rolled polymer, etc.

Cricut Expression 2: Cricut Expression 2, like the Cricut Expression, also cuts a wide collection of materials. The cartridges are often expensive; however, they can work without a cartridge if connected to a computer with the correct software.

Cricut Explore: This is another popular Cricut Machine that can cut over 100 materials. It cuts materials like glitter paper, cork, bonded fabric, etc. It is not the quietest nor the fastest, but it serves more and is beginner friendly. It could be more efficient and save stress, time, and money.

Cricut Explore 1: This Cricut is majorly designed for DIY crafts and projects; it uploads and cuts your images. It can work without cartridges or dies.

Cricut Explore Air: Similar to Cricut Explore 1, it is also designed for DIY crafts and projects.

Cricut Explore Air 2: This a DIY cutting machine for all crafts used to create customized cards, home decor, and more

Cricut Maker: Cricut Maker is designed with the widest variety of tools for cutting, scoring, writing, and adding decorative effects; it gives a perfect cut to intricate shapes in materials like poster board, cardstock, vinyl, etc.

What Can I Make With Cricut?

Cricut Machines have further simplified so much the work of cutting. Having Cricut Machines that can cut different types and sizes of materials has brought a lot of ease.

Cricut Machines can be used for various purposes, cutting different materials, including foods. It is used to cut materials of different qualities and sizes to be used in many craft projects.

It is used in customizing stickers and pantry labels, vinyl decals for car windows, designing handmade greeting cards, making leather eating and bracelet, and printing T-shirts and onesies. It is also used for monograms for a mug, a tumbler, or a cup, cutting fabrics, wood, and leather.

How Does Cricut Machine Work?

The Cricut machine works by connecting it to your computer or smartphone via Bluetooth or cable. Once it's connected, you can then create or download your designs. In addition, the machine is designed with software called '***Design Space***' which enables you to edit and adapt designs before cutting them out.

What Cricut Machines Are Out There Right Now?

There are many Cricut machines in the market, and our use of any Cricut Machine depends on one kind of project you want to do. Examples are Cricut Explore 2, Cricut Maker, Cricut Joy, Cricut easy press 2, Cricut Explore 3, Cricut Mini, Cricut Cake, Cricut Create, Cricut Maker 3, etc.

In conclusion, Cricut Machine is a machine made easy to remedy stress, inefficiency, and unsatisfied results. It has served lots of cutting purposes.

CHAPTER TWO
Cricut Buying Guide

Cricut Maker 3 is a machine designed to serve some specific purposes; therefore, it is not something one can buy randomly or impulsively. The purpose of buying must be well stated before proceeding to the market, as there are several alternatives you can consider before making any purchase.

Although there are several brands of Cricut machines in the market, such as Cricut Explore 2, Cricut Maker, Cricut Explore air, etc. The Cricut maker 3 has distinguished itself due to its design and decorative ability, smart tools, cutting features, and ability to cut several materials.

NOTE: *It is important to know that Cricut Maker 3 is expensive. The reason for its high cost can be attributed to its various types and smart tools.*

Cricut Maker 3 can be used to cut over 300 materials. Its tool system is smart and adaptive, making it possible to switch out up to 13 different tools to cut. It also enables its user to score, draw, deboss, engrave and foil a wide range of materials.

It can also cut designs for any project, giving you access to work mat-free; that is, you can work continuously on a project up to 12 feet in length. Cricut Maker 3 is compacted with some smart tools which were absent in the original version.

There are three very important questions you should answer before deciding which Cricut machine is best to go for; these questions include; How frequently do you wish to use this machine? How much can you afford to spend?

Finally, where do you want to store/keep this machine? The accurate answers you can provide to these questions will guide you in making the best choice of a Cricut machine. There are many choices that need to be seriously considered.

Different Cricut Machines In The Market Today

It is important to know that many Cricut Machines are in the market today. As time evolves, new technologies are invented to simplify Cricut's easy usage and efficacy further. Some latest Cricut Machines one can find in the market today include;

Cricut Maker 3:

Cricut Maker 3 is the latest and one of the best-selling Cricut in the market today. It was introduced to the series of Cricut Machines in the year 2021 in June. It is still rated as the latest version of the Cricut Machine, with different intelligent tools to draw, design, engrave and cut a wide range of materials.

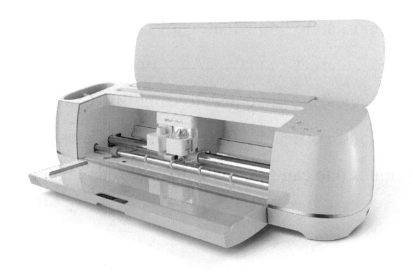

It cuts 300+ types of materials, including; leather, wood, and fabric. It accepts more than Twelve tools for cutting, writing, debossing, engraving, scoring, foiling, and lots more; it has a double tool holder. The Cricut Maker 3 tool system is adaptive, cutting with pressure and more precision.

Cricut Explore 3:

Cricut Explore 3 is an intermediate option among the best-selling Cricut in the market. It was introduced together with the Cricut Maker 3 in the year 2021 in June, and this series of Cricut have further interphases the previous Cricut Maker and Cricut Explore Air 2 with more distinctive features. It can cut over 100+ materials; it accepts two types of tools for cutting, writing, scoring, and foiling.

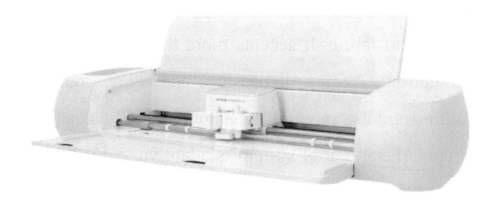

Cricut Explore Air 2:

Cricut Explore Air 2 is another series of Cricut Explore Machines which is gradually phasing out due to the introduction of the Explore 3 and Maker 3 series. This version of Cricut machine does not permit *"matless cutting."*

Cricut Maker:

Cricut Maker is the Original version of Cricut Maker 3. The difference between the Cricut Maker and the Cricut Maker 3 is that the Cricut Maker 3 works with a brilliant material, which was absent in the original Cricut Maker.

Cricut Joy:

Cricut Joy is the most portable version of the Cricut Machine with a smaller footprint; it is user-friendly and can occupy a small space. It weighs 4 pounds and measures eight by 5. It cuts materials like; iron-on vinyl, paper, adhesive vinyl, and some thin leather sheets.

Cricut Joy cuts 20+ types of materials; it can only accept two types of tools for cutting and writing. The maximum size a Cricut joy can cut on a roll of bright material is 4.5 by 12 with 5.5 wide rolls of smart materials compatibility.

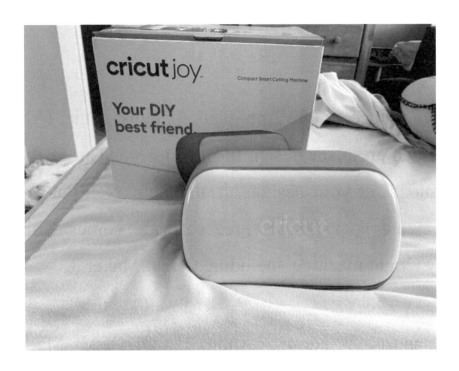

Cricut Joy uses a compatible mat card, which makes folded cards. It does not work well with an adhesive system. It uses free design space software. However, the print and cut project is not compatible with Cricut Joy, but it is the cheapest of all the Cricut series.

Design Space

Design Space is an App that contains some free unlimited pre-made design files, which you can easily download for your designs. It also helps you upload and create your design. Free software comes with every Cricut machine, including Cricut Maker 3.

It supports Windows, Android, iOs, and Mac. Unfortunately, it is also not supported on LINUX computers, Chromebook, or Unix. Design Space helps keep your designs in one place, saving you from exporting your designs.

The Design Space works with the Cricut Explore series, the Cricut Maker series, and Cricut Joy. For the first month of using the Design space, you don't need to pay for any subscription, as you will be given Cricut access.

However, you will subsequently be **charged a $9.99 monthly subscription fee** to access Design Space's unlimited features.

Cheat Sheet

A cheat Sheet is a free sheet of paper containing some guidelines on properly using the Cricut machine. It contains basic information to assist the Cricut user. In addition, Cricut Maker 3 has a cheat sheet to guide the user through its pros and cons. This cheat sheet guides you on the function of the Cricut and helps you navigate the design space confidently.

- The cheat sheet is organized to help the user learn and remember the functions and the names of everything that pertains to the Cricut.
- If you are new to the Cricut Maker 3, the cheat sheet will help you learn how to download your image, upload images, create your designs, and cut and print properly to get the desired result.

CHAPTER THREE

Getting Started

The new Cricut Maker 3 Machine is a simple DIY (*do it yourself*) machine. It is effortless to operate, and you can learn as many designs quickly. In this chapter, you will learn how to start with the Cricut maker 3.

Unboxing Cricut Maker 3

Unboxing a Cricut Maker 3 may come with huge expectations and curiosity to see what's hidden inside the bag. But the interesting thing is; unboxing your Cricut Maker helps you learn more about how to repack/store your Cricut after use.

Also, it helps you learn properly about the protocol of setting and fixing your Cricut machine for use. Here is how to unbox the Cricut Maker 3;

- Get your Cricut Machine, and place it on a flat surface. (*Ensure the surface is tidy to avoid mixing up your Cricut packages with other materials*).

- Gradually pull open the box from the top, remove the "**envelope**" you'll see inside the box. (*The envelope contains a sample of Cricut smart vinyl for your first cutting experience, a quick start guide, and a warranty and safety card*).

Envelop

- Pull out the cardboard inserted at both edges of the box and keep them aside.

- Remove the **"Smart Materials,"** which include a sheet of smart vinyl, transfer tape, a sheet of smart iron-on, and a piece of smart paper sticker cardstock. (*These smart materials distinguish Cricut Maker 3 from other versions of Cricut machines*).

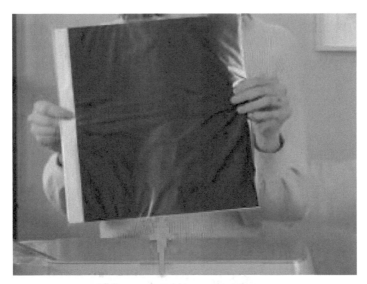

Smart Materials

- The next package in the box is the "**Cricut Machine**." Gradually pull it out and place it on the surface. The Cricut Maker 3 is packaged with a premium Fine-point blade.

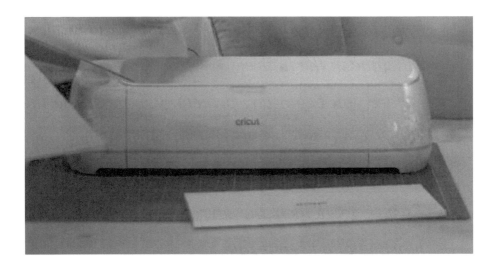

- Beneath the Machine is a "**USB Cable**" and "**Power Adapter**."

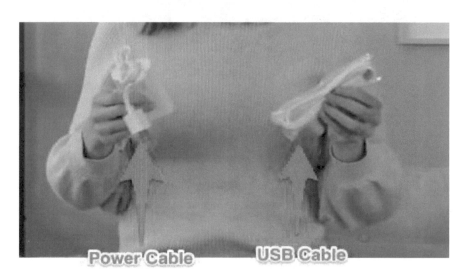

TIP: Here are some unboxing tips you should follow;

- *The Cricut Maker 3 box and the cardboard inserted at both edges of the box should be safely kept in case you want to resell your Cricut Machine in the future.*

- *Before you begin any project, you must use the smart materials as a trial to ensure that your Cricut Maker 3 is operating brilliantly.*

- *Ensure to detach the styrofoam from the tool housing and keep it safe.*

Anatomy of the Cricut Maker 3

In this section, you will be learning about the different components of the Cricut Maker 3. So, let's get started;

BUTTONS:

The right-hand side of the Machine has four buttons;

1. **Power Button:** The power button is used to power on and off the Cricut Maker 3.

2. **Load/Unload Button:** This button is used to feed the mat in and out of the Cricut machine.

3. **Start Button:** This is also known as the Go button or C button. You press this button to start your project.

4. **Pause Button:** This button used to stop a project during the cutting process temporarily.

STORAGE COMPARTMENT:

This compartment can be used to store and organize your equipment. It is very important when you are about to begin a project, as it holds the materials for you when the machine is cutting.

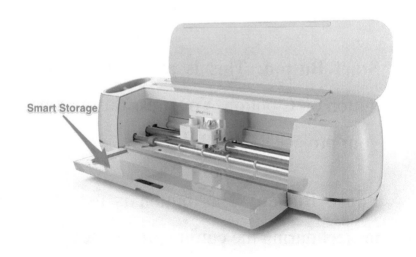

TABLET SLOT:

The tablet slot is used to hold your phone and tablet. Thus making it easier to pull up Design space while crafting or making designs.

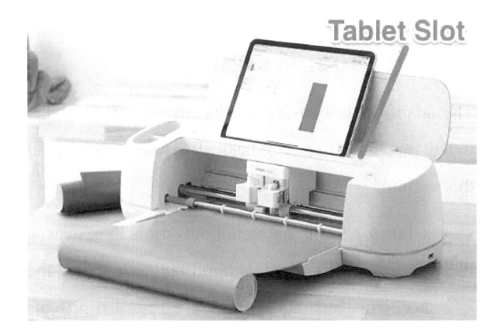

SMART STORAGE:

On the left of the Cricut is a smart storage cup that is lined with a silicone layer. The lining of this layer makes it best to store your blades without worrying about any damage.

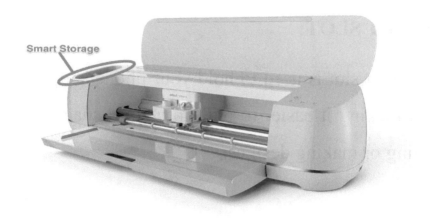

Smart Storage

ADAPTIVE TOOL SYSTEM:

The adaptive tool system is the driving force of the Cricut machine. There are basically two major tools in this section;

- **Clamp A:** This segment holds tools like; pens, a scoring stylus, etc. It is important to note that the accessory adapter comes pre-installed in this segment.
- **Clamp B:** This is where the Premium fine-point blade is installed. You can switch out with another tool by simply pulling on the clapse, removing the tools, putting in a new one, and securing it.

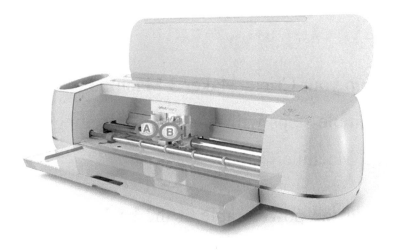

PORTS:

There is also a USB port carved at the side of the machine where you can charge your device. Also, there is the region where you can plug your power cable.

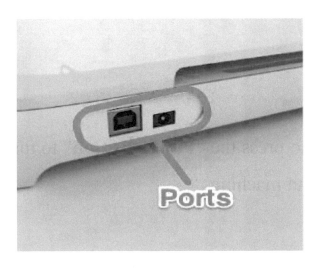

Initial Setup of Cricut Maker 3

Setting up your Cricut Maker 3 Machine is very easy. These simple steps will guide you in setting up your Maker 3 Machine.

- Plug the power cable at the back of the Cricut machine and connect it to a power outlet.

- Ensure to press the **"Power Button"** to turn ON the Cricut machine.

- The next step is to proceed to the official website of Cricut (https://design.cricut.com/#/setup) to get started with the initial setup.

- On the official website, you will be prompted to select a product type to set up. Ensure to select **"Cricut Machine."**

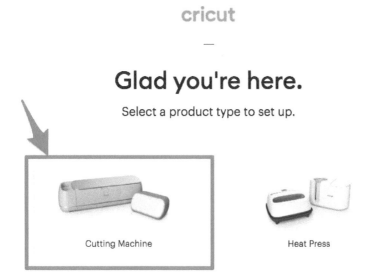

- Next, you will need to select the product that you want to set up. Ensure to select **"Cricut Maker Family."**

- In the next section, you must agree to Cricut's Terms of Use and Privacy Policy. Ensure to tick the small box.

- After you have accepted the terms, you can select the "Download" button to install the Cricut app.

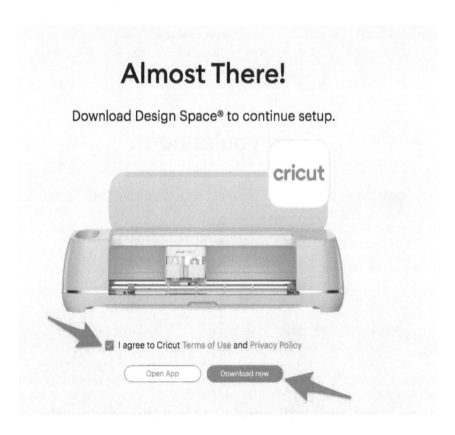

Almost There!

Download Design Space® to continue setup.

cricut

☑ I agree to Cricut Terms of Use and Privacy Policy

Open App   Download now

- After downloading and Installing the Cricut app, you will need to open it.

- A new window will open asking you the type of setup you want. Ensure to Select "**New product Setup**"

- The next step is to select the Cricut machine you are about to set up. Select "**Smart cutting machine**" and then click on "**Maker 3**." (*Ensure your connections are intact as you follow the prompt with the design space*).

- An on-screen window will guide you on how to set up your workspace and connect your Cricut to your Computer.

- To connect your Cricut to your computer, there are two methods; **Bluetooth** and **USB connection**.

- If you are using a USB connection, ensure to grab the USB Cable and connect one end to your Laptop and the other end to the Cricut machine.

- After connecting your computer and Cricut, ensure to select your method of connection on the Cricut app, and select "**Connect**."

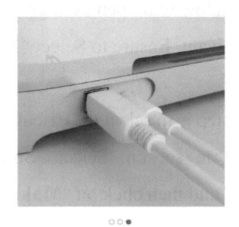

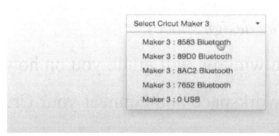

- Here, you will need to enter your Cricut ID or create a Cricut ID if you have not created one before to register your machine. (*After creating your Cricut ID, you can log into the design space*).

- In the next section, you will be prompted to "**Agree to the Terms of Use of Cricut**."

- Click on the "**Continue button**" to Update and Register your Cricut to your Design space account.

- After rebooting, your Design Space app will display a successful connection. Ensure to click on the "**Next**" button.

- Next, you will be prompted to "**Start your Free Trial**." You can skip this process by selecting "**No Thanks**."

- Next, you will be prompted to perform a "**Test Cut**."

- Pick the Image you would want to cut, and select the "**Next**" button.

- You will receive a message to confirm if the blade is in clamp B in the Cricut machine.

- After confirmation, you can click on the "**Next**" button.

- You will be directed to "**Insert your Smart Vinyl Under the Guide**."

- Then, click the "**Load button**" to feed the mat into the Cricut machine. Your Maker 3 will widen the materials and measure them to ensure enough space for cutting.

- Afterward, you can click the **"Start button"** to begin the cutting.

- When the cutting ends, click the **"Unload button"** to end the operation.

- After unloading the smart vinyl, proceed to weed out the designs.

Congratulations, your Cricut maker 3 is completely set. If you need an assistant at any point, you can contact Cricut customer care immediately and then continue afterward when you have properly received some guidelines.

TIP: *Cricut Access is a monthly or yearly subscription that grants you access to thousands of images, fonts, and projects.*

CHAPTER FOUR

Facts To Consider Before Crafting

Ignorance is very detrimental and can cause great damage in the end. Therefore, always crave knowledge and understand a thing before venturing into it. Crafting is one of the things you shouldn't do with a piece of half-baked knowledge.

So, you need to understand what crafting is all about, learn how to craft, understand which tools to use in crafting, and many more. In this chapter, you'll be informed about the essential facts before crafting with the Cricut Maker 3.

Crafting with a Cricut machine requires a whole lot to understand. However, you can explore and manifest your ideas if you understand the basics and intricate parts of the machine and the design space.

Tips To Know Before You Start Crafting

If you long to start making amazing designs yourself as soon as possible. Then, these tips are for you, as they will guide you to understand what crafting is all about and how to begin your journey. So here are some tips to know before you start crafting;

Purchase the Right Crafting Materials:

There are different materials to start preparing with as a beginner. These materials include; a pen, transfer tape, transparent vinyl, metallic marker and pen, foil iron-on, cardstock, poster board, glitter iron-on material, Cricut s paper sticker, dry erase vinyl, etc.

Ensure you have your Crafting tools ready before you begin to craft; you may need help to use them at the first craft; each of these tools is very necessary depending on the type of craft you are making.

TIP: *You can start with simple materials with ready-to-do projects.*

Organize your Crafting Space:

It is very important to create a considerable space for your crafting. A good space helps you craft excitedly. When you're crafting, a lot of tools and materials like colorful paints, vinyl, and ribbons will be around you, and it will be very dizzying to have these materials scattered around you in a space that is very compact.

Therefore, ensure you give enough space for your crafting skill. You can be inspired to create and organize your own craft space. A well-organized and spacious space will grant you happiness and clarity.

Familiarize Yourself with the Cricut Machine:

The Cricut Machines are designed for crafters, whether for individual or commercial purposes. Cricut Machines have unique structures and tools that make crafting easier and faster.

Cricut Machines work with electricity; it needs to be connected to a laptop or a smartphone, enabling you to create your design ID and access the design space. Spend time familiarizing yourself with the Cricut crafting machine and learning about the intricate parts and functions.

The impressive thing about the Cricut machine is that it guides you through each step; it helps you to choose better materials, load mats, and suitable blades.

Manage your crafting materials:

Always avoid waste, and ensure that YOUR materials are appropriately used. The design space helps to align the materials before cutting, so there'll be no waste.

There are times you'll have to reuse some of the materials. Materials like transfer tape can be reused. There are many other ways to reuse crafting materials. Some leftover crafting materials, like vinyl; fabrics, can be reused in future projects.

To save materials, many people have spent more money on blades than they should. They've never thought of sharpening it. A blade can be sharpened and used again instead of discarding it to get a new one. These simple facts will save you tons of money and time.

When working with intricate vinyl designs or lettering, use transfer paper. If you can also measure and cut your materials very well before placing them on the mat, it will also help preserve them. The transfer paper can also be reused.

Double-check your settings and make sure you do test work before cutting. It helps you to ensure that your grounds are aligned with suitable materials to avoid ruining your mat.

Study the Cheat Sheet:

Like every product the Cricut maker 3 has a cheat sheet, which serves as a directive on the use of the product for an excellent crafting experience.

This paper teaches you how to keep your crafting and the necessary materials. It teaches you shortcuts to maneuver through some software. Pay attention to the cheat sheet as you begin your crafting.

The cheat sheet will also help you to understand your settings to avoid deficit results. For example, It lets you know the material settings to choose from and the weight of your cardstock.

Thoroughly going through the cheat sheet will enable you to know which setting to use for the glitter cardstock and the standard cardstock. It also teaches you how to correctly remove your paper craft to avoid damaging your paper craft.

TIP: *Please only read the cheat sheet after using the crafting machine; instead, try to go through it before starting any project, as this will help you to avoid some mistakes.*

Understand the Design Space:

Use the design space often and understand how it works. If you are graphically inclined, the design space might be one of the places you'll get along with, and you should start creating your designs immediately. But I suggest you learn how to use design space first. Also, remember to customize your canvas in the design space.

Sort for more information online:

It is vital to visit the YouTube channel often for videos on some crucial tips. For example, Cricut YouTube channel, you'll learn more about how to set up your Cricut and craft with different materials. It also has some DIY videos for some specific tasks.

Learn from your Mistakes:

For a first-timer, you are bound to make a series of mistakes when crafting with design space and printing with the Cricut maker 3. Sometimes, it may be frustrating, and you will be annoyed. However, the key to overcoming frustration is managing your expectations and avoiding the perfectionist mentality.

CHAPTER FIVE

Cricut Design Space

Cricut design space is a unique software that enables a Cricut user to design and print out their desired design with the Cricut. With this software on your PC or iOS devices, you can channel your inner creative designs. This chapter will teach you how to use the Cricut Design Space.

Importance of Design Space:

Cricut design space is one of the essential tools in maximizing the Cricut machine, and it's like an ingredient that spices up your design in the Cricut. The following are some importance of Cricut's design space;

- It makes Cricut set-up easy.

- It's an intelligent tool that helps the Cricut user to create beautiful designs that the Cricut machine will cut. It also enables the user to download pre-designed images.

- With Cricut design space, you can modify the designs to your taste.

- Customization is also one of the features possible with the Cricut. Cricut design space allows you to choose from various designs for the preferred image you want to cut.

- With Cricut design space, you can easily attain a satisfactory result.

In conclusion, the Cricut Design space is a tool that adds beauty to your material. It makes crafting stress-free and encourages quick delivery.

How to Install Design Space for Desktop

You may want to know how to get the design space into your device and get started with your design craft. It is easy, and before you begin your installation process, your desktop must be connected to a stable internet network. Here is how to go about the process;

- Open your *"**Browser Application**"* on your desktop.

- Type the following address on the address bar of your browser app; ***https.//design.cricut.com.***

- Select the *"**Download icon**"* and wait for the downloading process to be completed; the screen may change at the cause of the download, which might differ depending on the browser.

- Once the download is completed, click on the downloaded file to begin the installation.

- At this time, you might receive a pop-up notification asking you to trust the app; kindly select the "*Trust icon*." The installation process will begin by showing *"Installation in Progress*."

- Once the installation is done, click on the installed app and sign in with your Cricut ID and password. **Note:** Ensure you put in the correct ID and password

- At this point, the design space for the desktop icon will automatically be added to your desktop screen; click on the icon and choose pin or drag the icon to the taskbar to pin the shortcut within each reach.

- Now, you can enjoy your Cricut design space on your desktop.

- Ensure to constantly save each work done in the design space, especially before you exit the app, as it doesn't automatically save your work.

NOTE: You may only need to sign in if you want to use the design space; the app automatically saves and remembers your sign-in, except if you signed out of the last session.

How to Install Design Space for iOS device

Examples of iOS devices compatible with design space may include iPhones, iPads, Macs, etc. Other devices include; windows and Android. Design space installation for iOS devices is similar to that of desktop devices. Therefore, using an iOS device, you can install and enjoy your design space following these simple guides.

- Select the "*App Store icon*" on your iOS device and click on it to open. Once it's open, search for the Cricut design space.

- Select and download the Cricut design space

- A notification comes on requesting that you trust the app. Click the "*Trust icon*," and the installation begins.

- Enter your Cricut ID and password to continue verification.

- The Cricut design space app Will automatically be added to your iPhone's screen. Click the downloaded app and journey through your DIY crafts experience with your Cricut design space.

Note: You can also access Cricut design space offline. Once the app is downloaded, you can access the images offline.

How does the Design Space Look Like on a Desktop?

The design space has a different interface depending on the device you are using it on. On a desktop, most of the hidden features are made plain. For example, you will notice different panels; top, left, right, and the canvas area.

So, it is easy to use Design Space with a desktop, and all the editing and creative options are available. In addition, you can quickly import photos and edit them on design space.

How does the Design Space Look Like on an iOS Device?

Smartphones are an easy way to quickly design projects and send them to your Cricut machine for printing. So they come in handy in certain circumstances. The interface of design space on mobile devices is compacted.

Several features on the desktop mode are not present. However, you can still use this app on your mobile device to design anything of your choice.

CHAPTER SIX

Cricut Design Space for Beginners

After you install the software on your device, you can use it both online and offline to create and layout designs. The software offers a wide range of art and fonts for you to select from, or you can choose from pre-designed projects. Once you have finished setting up, you can access the main software, and the first thing you will see is the home screen.

Top Panel

The Design Space Canvas panel is divided into two sections. The first section enables you to save, label, and cut your projects. The second section allows you to control and edit the canvas content.

The top panel in the Design Space Canvas section is used for modifying and organizing canvas items. This panel allows you to choose the font style you want to use, as well as adjust sizes and align designs.

Edit Panel

The Edit bar in Design Space offers a variety of tools for modifying images and text, including Linetype, Fill, Size, Rotate, Mirror, and Position. Additionally, it provides a range of options for text layers, including line spacing, letter spacing, and font style. The panel also includes various other tools such as;

1. Undo & Redo: Everyone makes mistakes while working. These buttons can help fix them. If you accidentally create something you don't like or make a mistake, use the Undo button.

NOTE: If you accidentally remove or edit something you didn't mean to, use the Redo button.

2. Fill: Select a color or pattern to fill the Print Then Cut image layer. When the Cut Linetype is selected, this option becomes available.

- No fill – Indicates that no fill has been selected for the picture layer in question. The layer will just cut. After a fill has been applied, this command can be used to return the layer to a cut-only state.

- Print — Select "Print" to see the color and pattern options for Print Then Cut.

3. Fill Swatch: Click the Fill swatch to add more Fill properties to your picture layer.

4. Select & Deselect: Select or deselect all elements on the Canvas at the same time.

5. Edit: Use this drop-down menu to access popular editing tools such as Cut, Copy, and Paste.

- Cut - This command will remove an image from the Canvas to your clipboard so that you may paste it later.

- Copy – Copy an image to the clipboard for later use.

- Paste - Paste a clipboard item that has been copied or cut into the Canvas.

6. Align option: This option allows you to define the margin that will be used to align two or more items. Objects can be aligned to the left, right, top, or bottom, or have horizontal or vertical centers. You may also equally distribute your objects vertically or horizontally.

- Align Left: When this option is selected, all items will be aligned to the left. The one furthest to the left determines where all the other elements will move.

- Center Horizontal: This option will align your items horizontally, centering text and pictures fully.

- Align Right: When this option is selected, all of your items will be aligned to the right. The one furthest to the right will determine where all the other elements will travel.

- Align Top: This option will center all of your selected designs. The element closest to the top determines where all the other elements will go.

- Center Vertically: This feature will align your elements vertically. It's useful when you're working with columns and want them to be sorted and aligned.

- Align Bottom: This option will align all the designs you've chosen to the bottom.

7. Arrangement: If you are working on a canvas with multiple photos, text, and designs, the new elements you add will always be placed on top of the existing ones.

However, sometimes you may want to move certain elements to the front or back of the canvas. In such cases, you can use the arrange option to reorder the elements according to your preference.

The software will recognize the position of the selected element and provide you with options to move it to the front or back of the canvas. Using the arrange option, you can easily adjust the layering of your design elements within the canvas.

The "***Send to Back***" option moves the selected object to the bottom of the layer stack, making it the least visible in the Layers Panel. The "***Move Backward***" option will move the object down one layer in the stack, while "***Move Forward***" will move it up one layer.

The "*Send to Front*" option will move the chosen object to the top of the layer stack, making it the most visible in the Layers Panel.

8. Flip: This option allows you to flip an object horizontally or vertically. When you select the "Flip" option, you have the choice to flip the object horizontally or vertically.

Flipping horizontally will reverse the object left to right, while flipping vertically will reverse the object top to bottom. This can be useful for creating mirrored images or for adjusting the orientation of an object.

9. Size: Change the width or height of an item by entering an exact number or using the stepper to change the size by 0.1

10. Rotate: Change the angle of your item by entering an exact degree or by using the stepper to change the angle by one degree at a time.

11. More: Some screen resolutions will be too small to see all tools on the Edit bar. In this situation, a "More" drop-down menu will display.

Design Panel

The Design panel is a section of the interface of Cricut Design Space that allows you to browse and access pre-designed templates, shapes, and other elements that you can use in your projects. Here are some of the features that can be found in the design panel;

1. New: In Design Space, the "New" option allows you to create a new design or project from scratch. When you select this option in the design panel, a pop-up window will appear, offering you the choice to create a new design or project from scratch or to start a new project using a template.

2. Templates: In design space, templates refer to pre-designed layouts or designs that can be used as a starting point for creating a new design. Templates can be helpful for designers who are looking to save time and effort by using an existing structure as a foundation for their work.

3. Projects: This segment is where you have already made customs. This feature has several advantages, as it enables your Cricut machine to start cutting your project immediately. From here, you can choose your project and customize it as desired.

4. Images: There are large numbers of images in the Cricut Library Images. According to Cricut, an extensive collection of over 100,000 images can be used in any project of your choice.

5. Text: Text is an important aspect of every project. In the design space, you can add text to the Canvas area by clicking on the "Text" button. This will add the word "Text" to the canvas, which you can then replace with your desired text.

6. Shapes: This section is where you can select some basic shapes to add to your canvas. When you click this section, you will see certain shapes like circles, squares, triangles, and score lines.

7. Phrase: If you wish to add text to your project or want to find quotes or sentiments, click on the "Phrases" filter. This filter is similar to the "Images" filter, and some people may find it to be duplicative.

8. Upload: Create your own cuttable forms from uploaded images with the help of Design Space. Both vector and Basic pictures are the two options for file uploads. You can upload different file types ranging from .jpg, .gif, .png, .bmp, .svg, or .dxf image files.

Layers Panel

Design Space includes a variety of tools to assist you in customizing your photos. Group, Ungroup, Duplicate, Delete, Slice, Weld, Attach, Flatten, and Contour are all available in the Layers panel. Let's look at these options;

1. Group: Combine numerous layers, pictures, or text on the Canvas so that they move and resize together. This has no effect on how photos are put out on the cutting mats.

2. Ungroup: This option will ungroup any grouped layers that you pick on the canvas area or layers panel, allowing them to move and size independently on the canvas. Use this option if you need to change the size, font, or other properties of a specific element or layer in the group.

3. Duplicate - This will copy and paste an item to make multiples of the same item.

4. Delete: This option will remove any item that you have chosen on the canvas or in the layers panel.

5. Slice - Use this to separate two overlapping layers into different parts.

6. Weld - Join many layers to form a single object, eliminating any overlapping cut lines.

7. Attach/Detach - Attach to keep your items in place so that the objects on the cutting mat look exactly as they do on your Canvas. Detach removes connected layers so that they are no longer attached and may be cut, drawn, or scored independently of all other layers.

8. Flatten/Unflatten - Flatten converts any image to a printable image by combining all chosen layers into a single layer. Unflatten divides layers from a single printable image into separate printable layers.

9. Hide or unhide contour lines or cut lines on a layer using the Contour tool. To apply Contour, you must first Ungroup the image if it contains several layers.

The open eyeball icon shows that the layer is visible on the Canvas and will cut, draw, score, or print. Hide the selected layer by clicking the symbol. Hidden layers cannot be cut, drawn, scored, or printed. When you click the icon again, the layer appears on the design screen.

10. Linetype - The current Linetype of each layer will be displayed in the Layers panel for reference.

CHAPTER SEVEN

Design Space Tips and Tricks

Design Space in Cricut is like a spice that adds flavor to your design in the Cricut, and it's one of the most important tools for getting the most out of your Cricut machine. Here are a few tips that will be useful;

How to Link Cartridges in Design Space?

To link cartridges in Cricut Design Space, follow these steps:

- Log in to your Cricut account on the Cricut Design Space website.
- Click on the *"Menu"* icon in the top left corner of the screen and select *"Cartridges"* from the drop-down menu.
- Click on the *"Link a Cartridge"* button in the top right corner of the screen.

- Enter the code for your cartridge in the text field and click the *"Link"* button.

- If you have multiple cartridges to link, repeat this process for each cartridge.

- Once all of your cartridges are linked, you can access their images and fonts by clicking on the *"Images"* or *"Fonts"* tab in the top menu and selecting the desired cartridge from the drop-down menu.

- If you need to unlink a cartridge, simply click on the "Unlink" button next to the cartridge in the Cartridges menu.

How to use Color Sync Panel

In Cricut Design Space, the Color Sync panel allows you to match the colors of your project to a specific color palette or brand. To use the Color Sync panel:

- Open the project you want to work on in Cricut Design Space.

- Select the *"Canvas"* tab on the right side of the screen.

- Click on the *"Color Sync"* panel, which is located in the "Layers" section of the right sidebar.

- In the Color Sync panel, you will see a list of the colors used in your project, as well as a list of color palettes and brands that you can choose from.

- To match the colors in your project to a specific color palette or brand, select the palette or brand from the list.

- Cricut Design Space will automatically update the colors in your project to match the selected palette or brand.

- If you want to customize the colors in your project, you can click on any of the colors in the Color Sync panel to open the color picker and choose a different color.

- When you're finished, click "*Apply*" to save your changes.

How to Use Patterns in Cricut Design Space

Pattern is a feature used to fill any text or image layers in Cricut Design Space. It is important to know that there are numerous patterns in the Cricut Design Space pattern library. If you do not like any of the patterns, you can customize or upload your own pattern. Here is how to use patterns;

- Open the project you want to work on in Cricut Design Space.

- Select the "*Canvas*" tab on the right side of the screen.

- Click on the "*Layers*" panel in the right sidebar.

- In the Layers panel, select the layer that you want to apply a pattern to.

- Click on the "*Fill*" dropdown menu in the Layers panel, and select "*Pattern*."

- A list of available patterns will appear. Scroll through the list and select the pattern you want to use.

- The pattern will be applied to the selected layer.

- If you want to customize the pattern, click on the *"Customize"* button next to the pattern name. This will open the Pattern Options panel, where you can adjust the size, alignment, and orientation of the pattern.

- When you're finished, click *"Apply"* to save your changes.

How to Mirror Designs

During the heat transfer process, your iron-on design will be protected by the shiny, clear, heat-resistant liner that is attached to most iron-on materials. Your machine can only cut your pattern if the liner is facing down. Consequently, before you begin cutting, you'll want to make a mirror image of your design in Design Space. Here is how to go about the process;

- Once you have finished customizing your design and are ready to cut, click on the *"Make It"* button to proceed to the project preview.

- If you have any design elements intended for heat transfer, make sure to toggle the *"Mirror"* switch on for each load type. Then, click *"Continue"* to complete your cut.

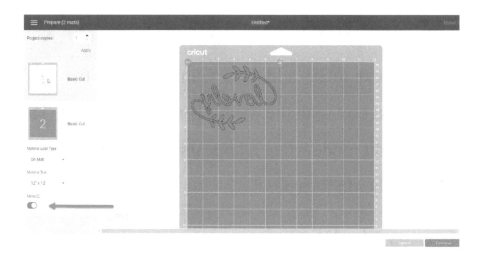

- If you forget to mirror your design and select a heat-transfer material setting, Design Space will remind you to do so. To fix this, click "*Edit*" and toggle the "*Mirror*" switch on, then select "*Done*." Repeat this process for each load type as needed.

- Once you have finished these steps, you are ready to cut your design.

Working with Text in Design Space

For new text to be added to Canvas, click the Text icon. A text box with the word "Text" highlighted. The text is in edit mode when it appears like this. To update your text, begin to type.

How to Modify Text:

The Edit mode ends if you click anywhere other than the text field, but making changes is simple;

- Double-click on your text, and choose Edit Text from the menu to add new words or make edits.
- Another option is to use the Edit menu's feature, or by right-clicking within the text box, you may cut, copy, and paste while the letter(s) are chosen.

How to Rotate Text

You can rotate text box on a canvas by using any corner handle of a bounding box or by entering a number in the Rotate input field in the Edit toolbar.

Allow the pointer to hover slightly beyond the corner handle of the bounding box while rotating until a curving arrow emerges. Rotate the text by clicking and dragging.

Sizing a Text

Text may be resized by dragging any corner handle on the bounding box or by entering values in the Size input boxes on the Edit toolbar. In the Edit toolbar, click the Lock symbol next to the width and height fields to unlock proportions so you may separately alter the width and height.

Resizing the text box

You don't have to modify the font size you've chosen to change the size of the box your text is in. Click and move the bounding box's main rectangular handles. By default, the text is aligned horizontally and vertically, but you may change the position of the text inside the text box by using the Alignment, Letter Space, and Line Space tools.

Text Wrapping

By default, just one line of text is put to the canvas. No line breaks are necessary; depending on the size of your text box, you may have your text wrap or flow to a new line.

Click and drag a center rectangular handle on the text box to move a word to a new line or bring a word back from the previous line. Your text box enters wrap mode as a result. Select Wrap Off from the Alignment menu to get out of the Wrap mode.

How to Curve Text

You may shape-shift your text into a circle with the Curve tool. To discover how to curve text in Design Space, go to this help page.

How to Delete Text

Use the delete keys on the keyboard to remove text from the Design Space.

Design Space Tips and Tricks

Here are a few tips and tricks for using Cricut Design Space:

- Use the **"Duplicate"** option to create multiple copies of an object quickly. This is especially useful for creating repeating patterns or for making small adjustments to multiple copies of the same object.

- Use the **"Group"** and **"Ungroup"** options to manipulate multiple objects as a single unit. This is useful for moving and resizing multiple objects at once.

- Use the **"Align"** and **"Distribute"** options to quickly and easily align multiple objects. These options allow you to align objects by their edges and centers or evenly distribute them across a page.

- Use the **"Weld"** option to merge two or more shapes into a single object. This is useful for creating more complex shapes or for combining text and images.

- Use the **"Contour"** option to cut out a shape or design from a larger object. This is useful for creating intricate cuts or for creating a "negative" version of a shape.

- Use the **"Flip"** option to quickly and easily reverse an object horizontally or vertically. This is useful for creating mirrored images or adjusting an object's orientation.

- Use the **"Fill"** and **"Outline"** options to add color to your designs. The Fill option allows you to add color to the inside of an object, while the Outline option allows you to add color to the outline of an object.

- Use the "**Layers**" panel to organize your designs and keep track of which objects are on top or behind others. This is especially useful for creating multi-layered designs or for adjusting the visibility of different objects.

CHAPTER EIGHT

Cricut Materials

The Cricut Maker 3 is a cutting machine that is capable of cutting a wide variety of materials, including paper, cardstock, vinyl, iron-on, fabric, leather, and more. It can also emboss and deboss certain materials.

After designing your project using the Design Space software, the next important element to consider is the choice of material to use. In this chapter, you will learn in detail the different materials you can use your Cricut Machine to cut.

Cardstock:

This is a thick, stiff paper that is commonly used for making invitations, business cards, and other paper crafts. It is typically made from recycled paper and is available in a variety of colors and finishes.

There are several reasons why cardstock is a popular material to use with the Cricut Maker 3 cutting machine. Here are a few reasons;

Sturdiness: Cardstock is a thicker and sturdier paper than regular copy paper, making it a good choice for projects that require extra stability. For example, cardstock is often used for invitations, business cards, and other paper crafts that need to hold their shape.

Versatility: Cardstock is available in a wide range of colors and finishes, including metallic, glossy, and matte. This makes it a versatile choice for creating a variety of projects, from invitations to greeting cards to home decor.

Precision cutting: The Cricut Maker 3 is capable of cutting precise, detailed shapes and designs, and cardstock is a good material to use for these types of projects because it is stiff and holds its shape well.

Durability: Cardstock is more durable than regular copy paper, making it a good choice for projects that will be handled or displayed frequently. For example, if you are making a banner or a sign, cardstock will be able to withstand the wear and tear of being hung up or displayed more easily than regular paper.

Overall, cardstock is a popular material to use with the Cricut Maker 3 because it is sturdy, versatile, and able to withstand handling and display. It is a good choice for a wide variety of projects, including invitations, business cards, home decor, and more.

The type of blade that you use with the Cricut Maker 3 will depend on the specific material that you are working with. For cardstock, it is generally recommended to use the **"Cricut Fine Point Blade."** This blade is designed for cutting precise, detailed shapes and is capable of cutting through cardstock and other thin to medium-weight materials with precision.

Vinyl:

Vinyl is a popular material to use with the Cricut Maker 3 cutting machine because it is versatile and easy to work with. Here are some reasons why you might choose to use vinyl with the Cricut Maker 3:

Decals and stickers: Vinyl is a popular choice for making decals and stickers because it is thin and flexible, making it easy to apply to a variety of surfaces. It is also available in a wide range of colors and finishes, including matte, glossy, and metallic.

Signs and banners: Vinyl is a durable material that is resistant to weathering, making it a good choice for outdoor signage and banners. It can be cut into a variety of shapes and sizes, making it a versatile choice for creating custom signs and banners.

Home decor: Vinyl is a popular choice for creating custom home decor items such as wall decals, pillows, and other decorative items. It is easy to work with and can be easily removed or repositioned without damaging surfaces.

Crafts and hobbies: Vinyl is a versatile material that is commonly used in a variety of crafts and hobbies, including scrapbooking, card making, and more. It is easy to cut and can be used to create a wide range of projects.

For vinyl, it is generally recommended to use the **"Cricut Premium Fine Point Blade."** Overall, vinyl is a popular choice for use with the Cricut Maker 3 because it is versatile, durable, and easy to work with. It is a good choice for a wide variety of projects, including decals, stickers, signs, home decor, and more.

Iron-on:

Iron-on is a type of heat-transfer material that can be used to create custom designs on fabric. It is a popular choice for use with the Cricut Maker 3 cutting machine because it is easy to use and can add a personal touch to a wide variety of projects. Here are some reasons why you might choose to use iron-on with the Cricut Maker 3:

Custom garments: Iron-on is a popular choice for creating custom garments such as t-shirts, sweatshirts, and more. It is easy to cut into a variety of shapes and sizes, and can be easily applied to fabric using an iron or heat press.

Home decor: Iron-on is a versatile material that can be used to create a wide variety of home decor items, such as pillows, towels, and more. It is easy to apply and can be removed or repositioned without damaging the fabric.

Crafts and hobbies: Iron-on is a popular choice for a wide variety of crafts and hobbies, including scrapbooking, card making, and more. It is available in a wide range of colors and finishes, including matte, glossy, and glitter, making it a versatile choice for adding a personal touch to projects.

Overall, iron-on is a popular choice for use with the Cricut Maker 3 because it is easy to use and can add a personal touch to a wide variety of projects, including custom garments, home decor, and crafts.

Fabric:

The Cricut Maker 3 can cut a variety of fabrics, including cotton, silk, and wool. It can also cut felt and foam, making it a versatile tool for creating custom garments, home decor, and other projects.

There are several reasons why you might choose to use fabrics with the Cricut Maker 3 cutting machine:

Custom garments: The Cricut Maker 3 is capable of cutting a variety of fabrics, including cotton, silk, and wool, making it a useful tool for creating custom garments such as dresses, skirts, and more.

Home decor: Fabric is a versatile material that can be used to create a wide variety of home decor items, such as throw pillows, curtains, and more. The Cricut Maker 3 can cut precise, detailed shapes and designs, making it a useful tool for creating custom home decor items.

Crafts and hobbies: Fabric is a popular choice for a wide variety of crafts and hobbies, including quilting, scrapbooking, and more. The Cricut Maker 3 can cut a variety of fabrics, making it a useful tool for creating custom projects.

Cost savings: Using the Cricut Maker 3 to cut fabric can be a cost-effective alternative to purchasing pre-cut fabric pieces or hiring a professional to do the cutting for you.

The type of blade that you use with the Cricut Maker 3 will depend on the specific fabric that you are working with. For most fabrics, it is generally recommended to use the **"Cricut Rotary Blade."**

This blade is designed for cutting precise, detailed shapes in soft materials such as fabrics, and is capable of cutting through a variety of fabrics with precision.

Leather:

The Cricut Maker 3 can cut thin to medium-weight leather, making it a useful tool for creating custom leather goods such as wallets, bags, and belts. Here are some reasons why you might choose to use leather with the Cricut Maker 3:

Custom leather goods: The Cricut Maker 3 is capable of cutting thin to medium-weight leather, making it a useful tool for creating custom leather goods such as wallets, bags, belts, and more.

Home decor: Leather is a durable and stylish material that can be used to create a wide variety of home decor items, such as coasters, placemats, and more. The Cricut Maker 3 can cut precise, detailed shapes and designs, making it a useful tool for creating custom home decor items.

Crafts and hobbies: Leather is a popular choice for a wide variety of crafts and hobbies, including jewelry making, scrapbooking, and more. The Cricut Maker 3 can cut a variety of leather types, making it a useful tool for creating custom projects.

For most leathers, it is generally recommended to use the Cricut Bonded Fabric Blade. This blade is designed for cutting thin to medium-weight fabrics and leathers. Overall, leather is a popular choice for use with the Cricut Maker 3 because it is durable, stylish, and can be used for a wide variety of projects.

Paper:

The Cricut Maker 3 can cut a variety of paper types, including standard copy paper, construction paper, and specialty papers such as watercolor paper and cardstock. Here are some reasons why you might choose to use paper with the Cricut Maker 3:

Greeting cards: The Cricut Maker 3 is capable of cutting precise, detailed shapes and designs, making it a useful tool for creating custom greeting cards.

Scrapbooking: Paper is a popular choice for scrapbooking because it is easy to cut and can be used to create a wide variety of projects. The Cricut Maker 3 can cut a variety of paper types, including standard copy paper, construction paper, and specialty papers such as watercolor paper and cardstock.

Home decor: Paper is a versatile material that can be used to create a wide variety of home decor items, such as wall art, garlands, and more. The Cricut Maker 3 can cut precise, detailed shapes and designs, making it a useful tool for creating custom home decor items.

Crafts and hobbies: Paper is a popular choice for a wide variety of crafts and hobbies, including card making, scrapbooking, and more. The Cricut Maker 3 can cut a variety of paper types, making it a useful tool for creating custom projects.

For most papers, it is generally recommended to use the Cricut Fine Point Blade. Overall, paper is a popular choice for use with the Cricut Maker 3 because it is versatile, easy to work with, and can be used for a wide variety of projects.

CHAPTER NINE

Selecting Blades

To achieve the finest results and the cleanest cuts, choosing the right blade for your project is key. However, for those new to Cricut, understanding the various blades and tools can be daunting. Not to worry, this chapter will help you navigate the different blades designed to work with specific Cricut machines. So get ready to become a blade master!

There are different blades you can use in the Cricut maker 3. Some of the blades are not compatible for certain materials due to their texture or smoothness. So, selecting the best blades for your project at all times is paramount.

Types of Cricut Blades

The Cricut Maker 3 is a versatile cutting machine that can be used with a variety of blades and tools for different materials and projects. Here is a list of some of the blades that are available for the Maker 3:

- Cricut Fine Point Blade
- QuickSwap Tools
- Knife Blade
- Rotary Blade

Fine-Point Blades

They are a set of blades designed to create the most detailed cuts possible in a wide range of thin to medium-weight fabrics. Cricut fine-point blades have a color-code, so you can tell which blade to use for your materials at a look. They are as follows;

Premium Fine Point Blade:

The Premium Fine Point Blade is ideal for cutting everything from paper, cardboard, and poster board to vinyl and iron-on. The Bonded Fabric Blade is used to cut appliqué from fabric that has a backing material attached to it.

Deep Point Blade:

The deep-point blade is another blade in the fine point family. It allows you to perform delicate cuts on a larger range of materials for your projects. Deep-Point blades are all black.

Bonded-Fabric Blade:

This blade provides all the functions of the Premium Fine-Point blade, but in a distinguishing pink color to match the FabricGrip mat.

QuickSwap Tools

QuickSwap Housing was designed specifically for Cricut Maker's adaptive tool system. It enables you to easily switch between scoring, debossing, engraving, and more.

Debossing Tip:

The Debossing Tip adds dimension to your work by creating crisp, intricate debossed designs in a range of materials.

Perforation Blade:

Perforation Blade provides perforation lines that are perfectly spaced, allowing for neat, uniform cutting.

Engraving Tip:

The Engraving Tip enables you to place designs on a range of materials, including soft metals and plastic.

Wavy Blade:

The Wavy Blade is a creative way to give any item a wavy decorative cut edge. By selecting the Wavy linetype in Cricut Design Space, you may convert standard cut lines into wavy lines.

Scoring and Double Scoring Wheel:

You can use the Scoring Wheel and the Double Scoring Wheel to make clean, precise fold lines on a variety of materials.

Knife Blade

With unmatched simplicity and safety, the extra-deep Knife Blade cuts through solid materials up to 2.5 mm (3/32") thick. It's best for medium-detail cuts in thicker materials including balsa wood, matboard, and chipboard. The maximum cut depth varies according to the material. The knife blade is housed in a silver housing with a gold gear at the top.

Rotary Blade

The rotary blade introduces highly adjustable, precise fabric cutting to the world of home sewing crafts. This tool allows you to cut cotton, canvas, poly blends, fleece, denim, felt, and other fabrics. This one-of-a-kind blade, with its gliding, rolling action, cuts through nearly any fabric quickly and perfectly.

Foil Transfer Tool

The Foil Transfer Tool is used in combination with Foil Transfer Sheets to provide a foil effect to projects on various materials. It comes with three replaceable tips: fine, medium, and bold, which are all appropriate for works ranging from basic outlines to complicated patterns. This tool is also compatible with Cricut Explore machines.

Scoring Stylus

The Scoring Stylus makes creases and fold lines in a variety of materials, including paper, cardstock, and poster board. This well-known tool is ideal for crafting cards, envelopes, boxes, and other 3D paper crafts.

How to Change a Knife Blade

Blades must be replaced at different intervals depending on the materials you use with your machine. Here is how to change a knife blade;

- Open Clamp B and remove the blade housing from your Cricut machine.
- For Fine-Point, Premium Fine-Point, Deep Point, and Deep-Cut blades: Gently press the pin on the top of the housing and carefully take the blade out from the bottom.
- Remove the new blade's protective cover.
- Insert the blade in the housing. The new blade will be held in place by the magnet in the housing.
- Finally, close Clamp B after replacing the blade housing.

CHAPTER TEN

Maintaining Cricut Maker 3

Maintaining your Cricut Maker 3 can help extend its lifespan and ensure that it continues to perform at its best. Here are some tips for maintaining your Cricut Maker 3:

Keep it clean: Regularly dust and clean the surface of your Cricut Maker 3 to keep it free of debris and lint. Use a dry cloth to wipe down the machine and a damp cloth to clean the blade housing and rollers.

Use the correct blade: Always use the correct blade for the material you are working with to ensure that you get the best results and to prevent damage to the machine. Refer to the Cricut Maker 3 user manual for information on selecting and changing the blade.

Store it properly: When not in use, store your Cricut Maker 3 in a dry, dust-free area. Avoid storing it in direct sunlight or in a damp or humid environment.

Keep it updated: Make sure to keep your Cricut Maker 3 software up to date by regularly checking for and installing updates. This can help improve the performance and stability of the machine.

By following these tips, you can help ensure that your Cricut Maker 3 stays in top condition and continues to perform at its best.

How to Clean the Interior of Maker 3

To clean the interior of your Cricut Maker 3, follow these steps:

- Turn off the machine and unplug it from the power source.
- Remove any materials or tools from the machine.
- Use a dry cloth to dust and clean the surface of the machine, including the blade housing and rollers.
- Use a damp cloth to wipe down the blade housing and rollers. Be sure to remove any excess water or moisture from the blade housing and rollers to prevent damage to the machine.
- Allow the machine to dry completely before plugging it back in and turning it on.

- It is important to clean the interior of your Cricut Maker 3 regularly to keep it free of debris and lint, which can interfere with the performance of the machine.

- Avoid using any harsh chemicals or abrasive cleaners on the machine, as these can damage the surface or components.

- Always follow the instructions on cleaning and maintaining the machine.

CHAPTER ELEVEN

Cricut Projects

There are several projects that can be done with your Cricut maker 3. In this chapter, you will be learning about several cricut projects that you can complete in 2023. Here are 49 Cricut project ideas to get you started:

1. Custom t-shirts
2. Personalized mugs
3. Custom invitations
4. Wall decals
5. Paper flowers
6. Stenciled pillows
7. Custom phone cases
8. Fabric bags
9. Paper garlands
10. Embroidered patches
11. Scrapbook layouts

12. Personalized notebooks

13. Custom coasters

14. Wall art

15. Paper lanterns

16. Stenciled tote bags

17. Paper earrings

18. Custom gift tags

19. Monogrammed towels

20. Scrapbook paper wreaths

21. Fabric headbands

22. Custom magnets

23. Paper lantern garlands

24. Embroidered hats

25. Stenciled placemats

26. Fabric bows

27. Custom jewelry

28. Scrapbook paper garlands

29. Personalized pens

30. Custom keychains

31. Wall decals for kids' rooms

32. Paper lantern mobile

33. Embroidered patches for jean jackets

34. Custom postcards

35. Scrapbook paper flowers

36. Fabric bows for hair

37. Monogrammed wine glasses

38. Custom gift wrap

39. Wall art for the kitchen

40. Paper lantern party decorations

41. Stenciled pillowcases

42. Fabric headbands for kids

43. Custom stickers

44. Scrapbook paper garlands for parties

45. Personalized pencil cases

46. Custom bookmarks

47. Wall decals for the bathroom

48. Paper lanterns for weddings

49. Embroidered

How to make Mugs with Cricut Maker 3

To make mugs with the Cricut Maker 3, you will need the following materials:

- A Cricut Maker 3 cutting machine
- A ceramic mug
- Permanent vinyl
- A Cricut fine point blade
- A Cricut transfer tape
- A Cricut weeding tool

Follow these steps to make a mug with the Cricut Maker 3:

Design your mug: Use the Cricut Design Space software to design the artwork or text that you want to apply to your mug. Select the "vinyl" material setting in the software and size your design to fit the mug.

Cut the vinyl: Load the permanent vinyl onto the cutting mat and insert it into the Cricut Maker 3. Select the "vinyl" material setting on the machine and follow the prompts on the display screen to cut the design. Use the Cricut fine point blade for best results.

Weed the design: Once the design is cut, use the Cricut weeding tool to remove the excess vinyl from around the design. Leave the actual design on the backing paper.

Transfer the design: Place the transfer tape over the design, smoothing it down to ensure that it sticks to the design. Use the Cricut weeding tool to lift the design off of the backing paper and onto the transfer tape.

Apply the design to the mug: Carefully place the design onto the mug, making sure that it is centered and straight. Use a scraper tool or the edge of a credit card to smooth down the design and ensure that it adheres to the mug.

Remove the transfer tape: Slowly peel away the transfer tape, leaving the design on the mug. If any areas of the design lift up with the tape, use the scraper tool or credit card to smooth them down again.

Cure the vinyl: Place the mug in a cool oven and set the oven to 350 degrees Fahrenheit. Once the oven reaches temperature, bake the mug for 30 minutes. Turn off the oven and allow the mug to cool inside the oven for at least an hour before removing it.

Your mug is now ready to use! Hand wash the mug to preserve the design. Do not microwave the mug or put it in the dishwasher.

How to Make Stenciled Pillowcases

To make stenciled pillowcases with the Cricut Maker 3, you will need the following materials:

- A Cricut Maker 3 cutting machine
- A pillowcase
- Stencil material or adhesive vinyl
- Fabric paint
- A Cricut fine point blade
- A Cricut weeding tool

Follow these steps to make a stenciled pillowcase with the Cricut Maker 3:

Design your stencil: Use the Cricut Design Space software to design the stencil that you want to use on your pillowcase. Select the "stencil material" or "adhesive vinyl" material setting in the software and size your design to fit the pillowcase.

Cut the stencil: Load the stencil material or adhesive vinyl onto the cutting mat and insert it into the Cricut Maker 3. Select the appropriate material setting on the machine and follow the prompts on the display screen to cut the design. Use the Cricut fine point blade for best results.

Weed the stencil: Once the stencil is cut, use the Cricut weeding tool to remove the excess material from around the design. Leave the actual design on the backing paper.

Transfer the stencil to the pillowcase: Place the stencil onto the pillowcase, making sure that it is centered and straight. Use a scraper tool or the edge of a credit card to smooth down the stencil and ensure that it adheres to the fabric.

Apply the paint: Use a foam brush or stencil brush to apply the fabric paint over the stencil, making sure to fill in all of the open areas. Use a light, even coat of paint to avoid drips or smudges.

Remove the stencil: Once the paint has dried completely, carefully peel away the stencil, leaving the design on the pillowcase. If any areas of the design lift up with the stencil, use a small paintbrush to touch them up.

Allow the paint to dry: Allow the paint to dry completely before using the pillowcase.

Your stenciled pillowcase is now ready to use! Wash the pillowcase according to the instructions on the fabric paint packaging. Do not dry the pillowcase in the dryer until the paint has fully cured, which may take several days.

How to make Custom t-shirts

To make custom t-shirts with the Cricut Maker 3, you will need the following materials:

- A Cricut Maker 3 cutting machine
- A t-shirt
- Iron-on vinyl
- An iron or heat press
- A Cricut fine point blade
- A Cricut weeding tool

Follow these steps to make a custom t-shirt with the Cricut Maker 3:

Design your t-shirt: Use the Cricut Design Space software to design the artwork or text that you want to apply to your t-shirt. Select the "iron-on" material setting in the software and size your design to fit the t-shirt.

Cut the iron-on vinyl: Load the iron-on vinyl onto the cutting mat and insert it into the Cricut Maker 3. Select the "iron-on" material setting on the machine and follow the prompts on the display screen to cut the design. Use the Cricut fine point blade for best results.

Weed the design: Once the design is cut, use the Cricut weeding tool to remove the excess vinyl from around the design. Leave the actual design on the backing paper.

Heat up the iron or heat press: Set the iron or heat press to the appropriate temperature and heat setting for the type of iron-on vinyl that you are using. Refer to the manufacturer's instructions for specific temperature and heat settings.

Preheat the t-shirt: Place the t-shirt onto an ironing board or other flat surface, with the front of the t-shirt facing up. Preheat the t-shirt by pressing the iron onto the surface of the shirt for about 10 seconds.

Apply the design: Place the iron-on design onto the t-shirt, making sure that it is centered and straight. Cover the design with a pressing cloth or a piece of parchment paper. Use the iron or heat press to apply heat and pressure to the design, following the manufacturer's instructions for the specific iron-on vinyl that you are using.

Remove the backing paper: Once the design has been applied, carefully peel away the backing paper, leaving the design on the t-shirt. If any areas of the design lift up with the paper, use the iron or heat press to apply additional heat and pressure to those areas.

Your custom t-shirt is now ready to wear! Follow the manufacturer's instructions for caring for the t-shirt to ensure that the design stays in place. Do not dry the t-shirt in the dryer until the iron-on vinyl has fully adhered to the fabric, which may take several hours or overnight.

How to make Fabric headbands

To make fabric headbands with the Cricut Maker 3, you will need the following materials:

- A Cricut Maker 3 cutting machine

- Fabric

- Heat-and-bond adhesive

- Elastic headband

- Scissors

- A Cricut rotary blade or bonded fabric blade

Follow these steps to make a fabric headband with the Cricut Maker 3:

Design your headband: Use the Cricut Design Space software to design the shape or pattern that you want to use for your headband. Select the "fabric" material setting in the software and size your design to fit the headband.

Cut the fabric: Load the fabric onto the cutting mat and insert it into the Cricut Maker 3. Select the "fabric" material setting on the machine and follow the prompts on the display screen to cut the design. Use the Cricut rotary blade or bonded fabric blade for best results.

Apply the heat-and-bond adhesive: Follow the manufacturer's instructions to apply the heat-and-bond adhesive to the back of the fabric. Be sure to cover the entire surface of the fabric with a thin, even layer of adhesive.

Cut the elastic headband: Measure and cut the elastic headband to the desired length. The headband should be long enough to fit around your head comfortably, with a little extra length to allow for overlap.

Assemble the headband: Place the elastic headband onto the back of the fabric, aligning the ends of the headband with the ends of the fabric. Use an iron to apply heat and pressure to the fabric, following the manufacturer's instructions for the heat-and-bond adhesive. Be sure to apply heat and pressure to the entire surface of the fabric to ensure that it adheres to the headband.

Trim the excess fabric: Once the fabric has cooled, use scissors to trim away any excess fabric from the edges of the headband.

Your fabric headband is now ready to wear! The headband can be worn as is, or you can add additional embellishments such as ribbons, beads, or buttons to personalize it.

How to make Custom invitations

To make custom invitations with the Cricut Maker 3, you will need the following materials:

- A Cricut Maker 3 cutting machine
- Cardstock or other paper
- Envelopes
- Glue or double-sided tape
- A Cricut fine point blade

Follow these steps to make custom invitations with the Cricut Maker 3:

Design your invitations: Use the Cricut Design Space software to design the artwork or text that you want to include on your invitations. Select the "paper" material setting in the software and size your design to fit the invitations.

Cut the invitations: Load the cardstock or paper onto the cutting mat and insert it into the Cricut Maker 3. Select the "paper" material setting on the machine and follow the prompts on the display screen to cut the design. Use the Cricut fine point blade for best results.

Assemble the invitations: Use glue or double-sided tape to attach the cut invitations to the envelopes. Follow the manufacturer's instructions for the adhesive that you are using.

Add any additional details: You can add additional details to your invitations such as ribbons, beads, or stamps to personalize them.

Your custom invitations are now ready to be mailed or hand-delivered to your guests. Be sure to follow proper etiquette when addressing and sending invitations, and include all necessary information such as the date, time, and location of the event.

What Next?

I truly appreciate you for getting to the end of the book. Undoubtedly, your reading experience has been seamless, and you can better understand the Cricut Maker 3.

If that has been your experience, I would be highly grateful if you wrote a reader review on the book's product page where you purchased the book. Every book my team and I produce are like our children, and we want to know how well it functions in the real world.

I always read my readers' comments because they tell me where I need to improve to enhance their experience. So, feel free to rate the book honestly and write a constructive evaluation, as it means so much to my team and me.

ABOUT BOOK

Are you ready to take your creativity to the next level? The Cricut Maker 3 is the ultimate cutting machine for your DIY projects. From custom T-shirts to personalized invitations, the possibilities are endless with this versatile machine.

For beginners, understanding how to use the different range of blades and tools of the Cricut Maker 3 can take time and effort. In addition, the Cricut Design Space may look very confusing for first-timers.

With this book, you will understand the following;

Unboxing Cricut Maker 3: This book will teach you how to set up your brand new Maker 3 without any mistakes. You will also be guided on how to make your first project.

Mastering Design Space: The Cricut Maker 3 may look like complicated software. This book contains several chapters dedicated to explaining how to navigate the Design Space with tips and tricks.

Creating Projects: This book contains practical steps on how you can express your creativity. Different projects are highlighted in this book, and how to get started with them.

Maintaining Cricut Maker 3: Maintaining your Cricut Maker 3 can help extend its lifespan and ensure that it continues to perform at its best. This book contains several steps and tips for caring for your Cricut Maker 3.

So, whether you're a seasoned Cricut user or a beginner looking to learn the ropes, our book on Cricut Maker 3 has everything you need to get started. So why wait? Start creating today with Cricut Maker 3!

Made in United States
Troutdale, OR
12/28/2023

16519618R00086